Segwun

A Muskoka Tour

Segwun

A MUSKOKA TOUR

Richard Tatley

The BOSTON MILLS PRESS

For further information about the lore of the Muskoka lakes steamers, be sure to read

The Steamboat Era in the Muskokas, Volumes 1 and 2
Published by the Boston Mills Press, Erin, Ontario N0B 1T0
OR WATCH
The Day of the Steamboat (videocassette, 77 minutes duration)
and *Cruising on the Segwun* (videocassette, 40 minutes duration)
Available at the Muskoka Lakes Navigation Company office
and bookstores throughout Muskoka.

TITLE PAGE PHOTO: *RMS* Segwun *at Beaumaris, c. 1955. (The flagsgip* Sagamo *is approaching at left.)* MUSKOKA STEAMSHIP & HISTORICAL SOCIETY

PHOTO CREDIT KEY:
MS & HS — MUSKOKA STEAMSHIP & HISTORICAL SOCIETY
NAC — NATIONAL ARCHIVES OF CANADA
OA — ONTARIO ARCHIVES

FRONT & BACK COVER (wooden boats) PHOTOGRAPHS: John de Visser; OTHER BACK COVER PHOTOGRAPHS: Terry Hrynyk

Copyright © 1998 Richard Tatley

Published in 1998 by
Boston Mills Press
132 Main Street
Erin, Ontario
N0B 1T0
Tel 519-833-2407
Fax 519-833-2195
www.boston-mills.on.ca

Distributed in Canada by
General Distribution Services Inc.
30 Lesmill Road
Toronto, Canada M3B 2T6
Tel 416-445-3333
Fax 416-445-5967
e-mail gdsinc@genpub.com
TELEBOOK S1150391

Distributed in the United States by
General Distribution Services Inc.
85 River Rock Drive, Suite 202
Buffalo, New York 14207-2170
Toll-free 1-800-805-1083
Fax 1-800-481-6207
e-mail gdsinc@genpub.com
PUBNET 6307949

02 01 00 99 98   1 2 3 4 5

Cataloging in Publication Data

Tatley, Richard
Segwun: A Muskoka tour

ISBN 1-55046-233-4

1. Segwun (Steamboat). 2. Muskoka (Ont.: District Municipality)–
Description and Travel. 3. Mail steamers–Ontario–Muskoka (District
Municipality)–History. 4. Steamboats–Ontario–Muskoka (District
Municipalty)–History. I. Title

FC3095.M88T37 1998   917.13'16004   98-931131-7
F1059.M9T37 1998

Design by Gillian Stead
Printed in Canada

Beaumaris, Lake Muskoka. NAC

Contents

Scene on the West Arm, Lake Muskoka, c. 1895. OA

Muskoka Wharf Station, 1904.
Steam Yachts Wanda *(I),* Mildred *and* Rambler *at dock. Passenger steamers* Medora *and* Nipissing *at rear.* OA

The District of Muskoka

The modern District of Muskoka comprises about sixteen hundred square miles of rocks and trees and lakes and islands, all set within the rugged grandeur of the Canadian Shield. It probably took its name from an Ojibwa chief named Mesqua-Ukee (or Yellowhead), who supported the British during the War of 1812. Mesqua-Ukee often fished and trapped in this area.

Until the 1850s the region was a vast Native hunting ground, virtually unknown to Europeans, but in 1850 the Canadian government, seeking new lands for settlers, began buying the lands north of the Severn River from the Ojibwas and building several colonization roads to open the country up for settlement. The results were often tragic, since most of Muskoka proved entirely unfit for farming. For a time steamers and stages helped to relieve the isolation of the region, and after 1875 the coming of the Northern Railway to Gravenhurst led to a boom in lumbering and sawmilling. By about 1910, however, the district had been logged out. Fortunately the rise of the resort hotels, which started in 1870 and really began flourishing in the 1880s and 1890s, rescued the region from destitution, and during the 1920s some light industry (including several boat-building plants) moved in to replace the forest industries. Muskoka became a separate district in 1888, with its capital at Bracebridge. Today it is Ontario's foremost cottage and recreation area, and its permanent population more than doubles every summer.

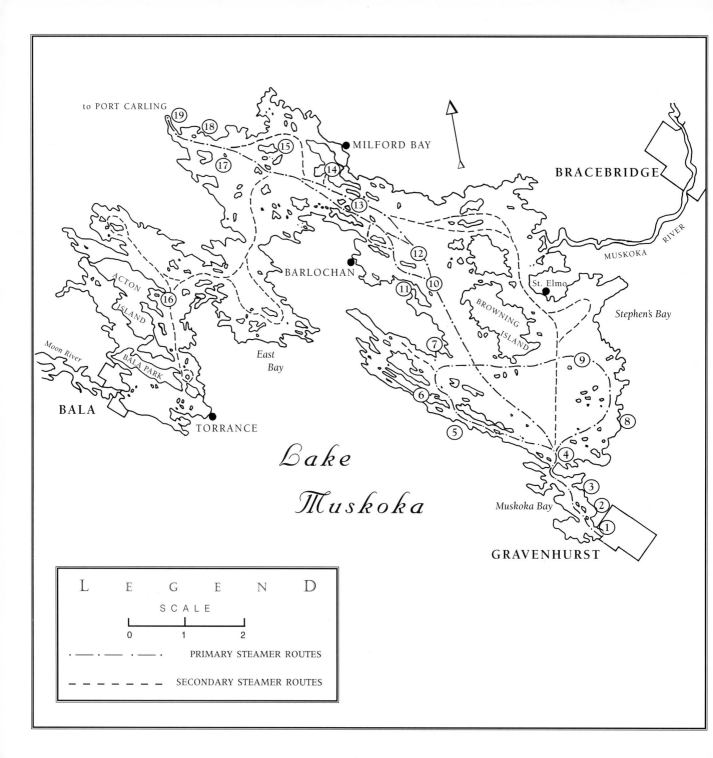

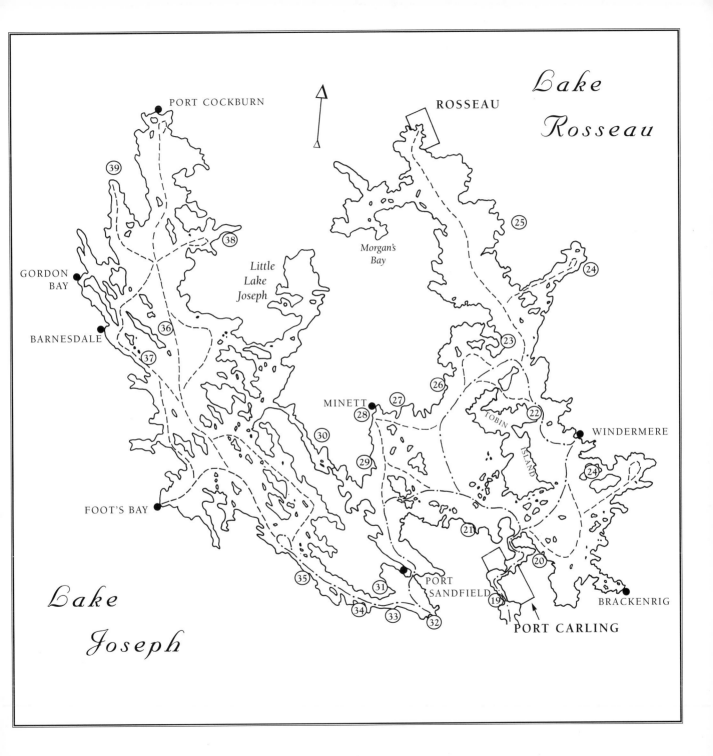

Lake Rosseau

PORT COCKBURN

ROSSEAU

㊲

㊳

Morgan's Bay

㉕

㉔

GORDON BAY

Little Lake Joseph

㊱

BARNESDALE

㊲

㉓

㉖

MINETT

㉗

TOBIN ISLAND

㉒

㉘

WINDERMERE

㉚

㉙

㉔

FOOT'S BAY

㉑

㉟

㉛

Lake Joseph

PORT SANDFIELD

㉜

㉝

㉞

⑳

⑲

PORT CARLING

BRACKENRIG

The RMS Segwun *and* Islander *dock at Beaumaris.* MS & HS

The RMS Segwun

The Royal Mail Steamship *Segwun* ("springtime" in Ojibwa) is the sole surviving ship of her kind still in commission in North America. She is Canada's only inland-waterway freight and passenger steamer still in regular service, conducting excursion cruises on the far-famed Muskoka lakes in central Ontario.

Back in the nineteenth century, when roads were terrible, railways scarce, and automobiles and motorboats unknown, steamboats were in their heyday. The *Segwun*, now unique, was then just one of a whole fleet of steamboats gliding up and down the Muskoka lakes ferrying passengers, supplies, and mail to all of the towns, villages, and resort hotels. Around 1910 the traffic was so heavy that the old Muskoka Lakes Navigation Company needed ten steamers to cope with the crowds arriving daily by train from Toronto! Similar fleets operated on many other waterways, including the Huntsville lakes, the Lake of Bays,

Georgian Bay, Lake Simcoe, and the Kawarthas. The lake steamers were so vital that no one could have imagined the Muskoka scene without them.

The *Segwun* is now more than a century old. She was first built of Welsh iron in the shipyards of Glasgow, Scotland, back in 1887, and shipped across to be assembled at Gravenhurst. She was originally a side-paddlewheel steamer called the *Nipissing*, and was once the flagship of the Muskoka fleet. In 1914 she was laid up following an engine breakdown, but in 1925 she was rebuilt as a twin-propeller ship and renamed *Segwun*. As such she became an auxiliary steamer, usually running from Bracebridge or Bala twice a day and connecting at Beaumaris with her sister ships, such as the *Sagamo*, *Cherokee*, and *Islander*. Sometimes she was also assigned the Lake Rosseau route, plying from Rosseau village and making connections at Port Carling.

The *Segwun* made her last trip in August 1958 and thus outlasted almost all the other passenger

Prime Minister Pierre Elliott Trudeau attends the launch of the partially restored RMS Segwun, *1974.* MS & HS

steamships in Canada. She escaped the scrapyards by being converted into a floating marine museum at Gravenhurst in 1962. Seven years later a restoration campaign was started to bring her back to full operating condition. After an eleven-year effort and a cost of $1,200,000, she was ready to reenter service in 1981. Today she is Muskoka's greatest tourist attraction and a major asset to the Ontario tourist economy, still plying in the gracious, elegant style of bygone times, and still running on coal and live steam. Length: 125 feet. Register tonnage: 168.39.

The Muskoka Lake Steamers

Steamers have been part of the Muskoka lakes scene almost from the beginnings of recorded history. They first appeared in pioneer times, back in 1866, and provided the original mechanized transport service throughout the district, hauling freight, passengers, and the royal mail, and also towing logs for the lumber companies. In the days when roads were mud-holes and railways nonexistent, steamboats were absolutely indispensable to settlers, merchants, and forwarders alike.

The first steamboat on the lakes was the *Wenonah*, a small wooden side-wheeler built at Gravenhurst in 1866. She plied regularly to Bracebridge, Tondern Island (Beaumaris), and the Indian Village (Port Carling) for twenty years, often facing storms, drifting logs, and un-discovered shoals. She was soon joined by other steamers, such as the *Waubamik* (1869), the *Nipissing* (1871), and the *Simcoe* (1875). By 1872 the construction of a lock at Port Carling and a canal at Port Sandfield removed all obstacles to navigation between Lake Muskoka and the upper Muskoka lakes (Rosseau and Joseph). The coming of the Northern Railway (now part of the Canadian National) to Gravenhurst and Muskoka Wharf in 1875 provided a direct link with Toronto. The railway was also a major spur to sawmilling and lumbering, and later to the growth of the tourist industry. By the 1880s resort hotels were springing up everywhere around the lakes, which in turn required more steamers to bring in the guests. In 1881 the steamer *Muskoka* was built, soon to be followed by the *Kenozha* (1883), *Oriole* (1886), and *Nipissing (II)* (1887, now the *Segwun*).

As the resort industry thrived, more steamers were built. In 1893 the opulent palace steamer *Medora* was built, in 1896 the *Ahmic,* and in 1900 the *Islander*. In 1906 and 1907 two splendid, steel-hulled palace steamers, the *Sagamo* and the *Cherokee,* joined the fleet which was now the largest on any inland waterway in Canada. In 1920 the Muskoka Lakes Navigation Company inaugurated the famous 100 Mile Cruise from Gravenhurst to the Natural Park on Little Lake

The Nipissing (II), *c. 1898.* OA

The Sagamo, *c. 1910.* NAC

Joseph. The majestic *Sagamo* always conducted the service from Gravenhurst, while the other ships acted as feeders, plying from such local ports as Bala, Rosseau, and Foot's Bay, and connecting at Beaumaris, Port Carling, and other places. In 1925 the *Segwun* was built out of the retired steamer *Nipissing* and usually assumed the Muskoka River route from Bracebridge.

With the onset of the Depression in 1930, the paving of the highways, and the spread of automobiles, trucks, and motorboats, the need for the steamers diminished, and ship after ship was withdrawn from service. The end came in 1958, when the *Segwun* and *Sagamo* sailed for the last time. While the other steamers went to the scrapyards (or were allowed to sink), the *Segwun* was fortunately spared, and after her stint as a museum ship she returned to active service in 1981. Today she is the last living link with a priceless part of our heritage.

STEAM YACHT WANDA III

The *Wanda III* is the largest and fastest steam yacht ever to ply on the Muskoka lakes. She has a triple-expansion steam engine and can do 20 knots. She was built in Toronto in 1915 for the Timothy Eaton family of department store fame, after her predecessor, the *Wanda II*, was lost in a boathouse fire. The *Wanda III* was used mainly to conduct pleasure cruises: Mrs. Eaton used to entertain her friends with tea, and cucumber sandwiches on afternoon outings from the Eatons' summer estate at Windermere. In 1930, however, the *Wanda III* was sold and taken to the Lake of Bays to become a hotel yacht for Bigwin Inn. After 1949 she was acquired and partially restored by a local steam buff. In 1993 she was offered to the Muskoka Steamship & Historical Society of Gravenhurst and transported back to her original waters. Since then she has been completely refitted by the Muskoka Lakes Navigation Company (which operates the *Segwun*) and today the *Wanda III* conducts charter cruises with the same grace and elegance as in the days of the Eatons. Length: 94 feet. Tonnage: 37.54.

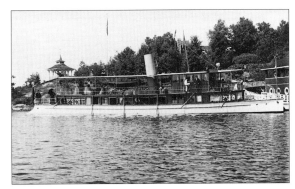

The *Wanda II at the Eaton family estate at Windermere.* NAC

Prime Minister and Madame Chrétien visiting the restored steam yacht Wanda III. MS & HS

The fleet at the Gravenhurst dockyards, (now Sagamo Park), May 1908. MS & HS

GRAVENHURST

The town of Gravenhurst, which prides itself on being the home port for the *Segwun*, was first settled in 1860, around a log tavern on the old Muskoka Road. With the coming of the steamboat service and a stage line to Washago (starting in 1866), it grew rapidly as a transshipping centre, a position confirmed by the arrival of the Northern Railway in 1875. After that, Gravenhurst became a booming lumber town, with so many saw and shingle mills that people dubbed it "Sawdust City." After the turn of the century it settled into a new role as a tourist town and cultural centre, aptly known as the Gateway to the Muskoka Lakes. Besides the *Segwun*, it is home to the Bethune Memorial Home (where the famous Dr. Norman Bethune was born), the Opera House, which hosts live summer theatre, and the "Barge" at Gull Lake Park, where concerts are performed. Population: c. 9,000.

1. MUSKOKA WHARF

The old Muskoka Wharf depot was built in a sheltered cove about a quarter of a mile west of the present Gravenhurst town wharf by the Northern Railway of Canada, back in 1875. For seventy-seven years trains from Toronto used to connect there with the Muskoka lake steamers. Thousands of passengers and huge consignments of freight and baggage were unloaded from the trains to the steamers and back again. By the turn of the century the Grand Trunk Railway (which absorbed the Northern in 1888) had to send up to five express trains a day to handle the rush.

Traffic began to decline during the Depression, and the old station, already abandoned by the railway, was demolished in 1959, after the steamers ceased operating. In 1992 a new depot, styled after the original and using the old Grand Trunk colours, was built at Sagamo Park, Gravenhurst, by the revived Muskoka Lakes Navigation Company. The new Muskoka Wharf serves as a ticket office and souvenir shop for the *Segwun*. An adjacent wing houses the RMS Segwun Heritage Centre, a small museum and interpretive centre used to introduce visitors to the ship and her proud past.

Muskoka Wharf Station, Gravenhurst, c. 1905. OA

2. ONTARIO FIRE COLLEGE

The Ontario Fire College is a prominent landmark on the east side of Muskoka Bay, about a mile north of the *Segwun*'s wharf. It was founded in 1955 and is now used to train firefighters from all over Canada and abroad. In recent years it has been expanded and upgraded. It is not unusual to see flames shooting from the tall, concrete towers on the grounds – they are used for practice fires.

3. GRAVENHURST SANATORIUM

The old Gravenhurst Sanatorium, or TB hospital, with the gazebo in front, was built in 1922 to replace an earlier building and commands a fine view from its lofty headland on Muskoka Bay. It was originally established in 1897, at a time when it was felt that the cool, bracing fresh air of Muskoka would benefit patients with respiratory diseases. At one time there were three such hospitals on the bay.

By the 1950s new drugs were developed for treating tuberculosis, and the sanatorium became obsolete. In 1960 it was shut down. It was promptly converted into the Muskoka Centre, for treating mentally handicapped people, but in 1994 the Centre was likewise closed, and today (1998) the building faces an uncertain future.

The Gravenhurst Sanatorium, 1897. OA

The Gravenhurst Narrows, Lake Muskoka, c. 1910. NAC

4. GRAVENHURST NARROWS

The Gravenhurst Narrows is the only channel linking Muskoka Bay with the main portion of Lake Muskoka and consequently it has seen a lot of boating traffic. It is well named in that it is barely 60 feet across at the narrowest point, and requires very careful navigation by large vessels like the *Segwun*. The beacon on Lighthouse Island, just beyond the Narrows, is the only one of its kind on Lake Muskoka. It was built in 1905. (Previously a coal-oil lantern was hung on a pole.) Originally a local settler was hired to set the beacon's lights every night; today it is electrified. It is an invaluable aid to navigation.

Steamers Medora, Muskoka *and* Nipissing (II) *leaving Gravenhurst, c.1904.* NAC

LAKE MUSKOKA

Lake Muskoka is the largest and southernmost of the major Muskoka lakes. It is about eighteen miles in length and about eight miles across at the widest point and very irregular in shape. Many of its waters are 150 feet deep, and at one point the depth is 210 feet. Lake Muskoka receives the waters of the two upper lakes, Lakes Rosseau and Joseph, which flow down into Lake Muskoka by way of the Indian River, around Port Carling. It also receives the waters of the Huntsville lakes and the Lake of Bays, which drain into eastern Lake Muskoka by way of the Muskoka River. Lake Muskoka drains westward, into Georgian Bay via the Moon and Musquash Rivers; the outlet is at the little town of Bala.

There are nearly 150 islands in Lake Muskoka. The largest, Browning Island, is several square miles in area; others are tiny. The lake was formed by meltwaters from the receding glaciers over nine thousand years ago, although the Ojibwas explained things differently. They say that, long ago, the great god Gitchi-Manitou had to do battle with his evil adversary, the Matchi-Manitou, who arose out of the waters of Lake Huron to fight him. Gitchi-Manitou tore up huge rocks and hurled them at his enemy, killing him. The rocks became the Thirty Thousand Islands of Georgian Bay, while the holes left behind became the Muskoka lakes.

5. SHADY LANE / WINDSOR GAP

The channel in western Lake Muskoka, between Rankin Island and the mainland shore, is commonly called Shady Lane, after a local side road which services some of the mainland cottages. Halfway up the channel is Greene's Rock Shoal, where a local man named Greene froze to death one winter night around 1926. Farther ahead is the Windsor Gap, between Rankin and Taylor Islands. It was likewise named for a local family of settlers. Within sight of the Windsor Gap is Campbell's Landing, founded by Peter B. Campbell around 1946. Campbell's Landing serves most of the island cottagers in the area and is now the largest marina on Lake Muskoka.

6. GLEN ECHO

Glen Echo Lodge, on the east side of Taylor Island (formerly called Island F), was once a regular calling place for the Muskoka steamers. The lodge grew out of the Island F Hotel, which catered mainly to lumbermen. In the 1920s it became Glen Echo and sometimes took up to sixty guests. The hotel was totally dependent on the lake steamers to bring in patrons and mail, although about 1934, after Highway 69 was rerouted close to the mainland shore, the proprietor built a scow ferry propelled by cables to bring guests and their cars to the island. Glen Echo was still a resort as late as 1972. Today it is a large summer cottage. Most of the old hotel building still stands.

7. POINT MONTCALM

Point Montcalm forms the southern tip of the headland of Walker's Point on western Lake Muskoka. It was named by David Lafraniere, a French-Canadian hotelkeeper from Gravenhurst, after General Montcalm, who was killed at the Battle of the Plains of Abraham in 1759, defending Quebec against the British. Mr. Lafraniere bought the point and built a small resort hotel called the Montcalm Villa around 1900. It burned in the winter of 1942. Today a magnificent log summer home occupies the site. Point Montcalm is located almost exactly at the forty-fifth parallel of latitude, which puts it halfway between the equator and the North Pole.

9. MUSKOKA SANDS

Muskoka Sands Inn is the only large resort hotel on southern Lake Muskoka. It stands adjacent to Muskoka Beach, a popular swimming park for the town of Gravenhurst, and the mouth of the Hoc-Roc River, which flows down from Gull Lake. The Sands was originally Muskoka Beach Inn and was established in 1926. It was never a steamer stop, since it was always readily accessible from Gravenhurst. Following a fire in 1959, it was rebuilt and became Muskoka Sands. The big hotel is a noted year-round conference centre, and has numerous condominiums in close proximity.

10. ELEANOR ISLAND

Eleanor Island, which lies in open water south of Browning Island, has the distinction of being the only bird sanctuary on Lake Muskoka. The sanctuary was proclaimed by the former Township of Muskoka in 1969, just before both were annexed to the Town of Gravenhurst. The preserve is intended to provide a safe nesting place for water birds, especially gulls and cormorants. No one is allowed to land there. One can easily see several nests high in the treetops used regularly by blue herons, which migrate south to the Carolinas in winter.

11. THE STONE MAN

The Stone Man stands at the north end of Nine Mile Island, off the headland of Walker's Point. He was built by cottagers in imitation of the rock cairns known as "stone men" (or *inukshuk*) that Inuit hunters in the Arctic barrens sometimes pile up to get the caribou herds accustomed to vertical objects, including men! The island was so named by the local boatmen long ago because it is located nine miles north of Gravenhurst.

12. WALKER'S POINT

Walker's Point was one of the earliest European settlements on Lake Muskoka. It was named for the family of Captain Harper Walker, a local boatman who arrived in 1869. Captain Walker built and operated several tugs and accepted contracts to tow logs for the lumber companies and move scow loads of freight and bulk cargoes for settlers and cottagers. The family home became the Walker House Hotel, a small resort and post office. The *Sagamo* made her last call at Walker's Point in 1957. A mile north of the point is Barlochan Bay, where the Barlochan post office was opened around 1910.

A summer cottage scene on the Muskoka Lakes, c. 1900. NAC

13. OLD WOMAN ISLAND

Old Woman Island lies in front of Barlochan Bay. According to legend it derives its curious name from an old Indian who is said to have carved a tree trunk at the south end of the island into the shape of a woman, long ago. Years later, when paddling past the site, he noted that the carving had become gnarled and twisted and bent, like a veritable "old woman." (Some attribute the statue to a romantic English sailor.) The name has been in use since the 1870s. Next to Old Woman Island is Stonewall Island, which is so thin in places that nothing holds it together except a string of giant boulders that looks very much like a stone wall.

14. MILLIONAIRES' ROW

"Millionaires' Row" is a local nickname for the large cottage community on the islands near Beaumaris in central Lake Muskoka. The millionaires were originally prosperous Americans, mostly from Pittsburgh and vicinity, who were attracted by advertisements circulated by the Muskoka Lakes Navigation Company and the Northern Railway, describing Muskoka as a sportsman's paradise. They began staying at the Beaumaris Hotel on Tondern Island (founded in 1883) and gradually started to buy some of the adjacent property for cottages. The first cottages were very modest affairs, but soon a spirit of "one-upmanship" began to set in, and in time some of these summer homes came to boast up to fifteen bedrooms, with quarters for servants. Many cottagers also built giant boathouses for their yachts. Some families have been coming to Millionaires' Row for five generations.

15. BEAUMARIS

The village of Beaumaris, on Tondern Island, has always been the focal point for Millionaires Row, and for decades it was the central meeting place for the Muskoka steamboats. It was named for Beaumaris, Wales.

Tondern Island was first settled and farmed around 1864. By 1874 a bridge linked it with the mainland. In 1883 Edward Prowse, an English settler, built the Beaumaris Hotel, directly facing the steamboat wharf. It grew rapidly and was soon taking two hundred guests, mainly Americans, while the Prowse farm became the Beaumaris Golf and Country Club. A store and church soon followed, as well as a yacht club. In 1945 the Beaumaris Hotel was torched by an arsonist, though with no loss of life. The golf course is still maintained, and the village still has a large marina.

The Sagamo *and* Islander *at Beaumaris, c. 1948.*   MS & HS

Cedar Wild, Milford Bay (now Pals of Muskoka). NAC

MILFORD BAY

The village of Milford Bay lies behind Beaumaris on the eastern shore of Lake Muskoka. It was once home to four resort hotels, including the Milford Bay House, Roseneath, and Cedar Wild, later called Milford Manor. Today only Elmhurst Lodge continues to take guests. Milford Bay still has a church, golf course, store, and community centre. Population: ca. 100.

16. SEVEN SISTERS ISLANDS

The Seven Sisters are a cluster of islands in northern Lake Muskoka. The largest, Keewaydin Island, once had a summer post office called Port Keewaydin. At the northern tip of Idylwild Island is a geological formation known as Indian Head Rock.

17. THE WEST ARM

The West Arm of Lake Muskoka extends about four miles west of the Seven Sisters before terminating at Bala Bay. Here stand the villages of Bala and Torrance. Bala Park Island, traversed by the Canadian National Railways, was once a coaling point for the lake steamers, while Acton Island, accessible from the mainland, was once the summer home of the late, noted broadcaster Gordon Sinclair. Several resorts once stood on the West Arm, including Rossclair, Pleasant View, and Wingberry House.

18. ONE TREE ISLAND

Tiny One Tree Island in northern Lake Muskoka once had a tall pine tree that could easily be spotted by the boat crews, making it a convenient checkpoint for navigation. In its vicinity, steamers would frequently stop and snub together to exchange freight and passengers mid-lake, using whistle signals to communicate. Nearby Horseshoe Island, so called because of its shape, is the most northerly in the lake.

One of many small islands in the Muskoka Lakes, this one on Lake Joseph.
MS & HS

19. SNUBBIN POINT

Snubbin Point is on the east side of the entrance to the Indian River. It was so named because, in the days of the big log drives, the lumbermen used to snub, or attach, the end of their log booms to an iron ring embedded in the rock. The booms in turn were used to collect and "bag" the logs floating down the Indian River, which were then towed to the mills at Gravenhurst. The logs were a serious nuisance to navigation, and sometimes the steamboat captains had to threaten to ram and break the booms to get the drivers to leave a passage clear.

20. INDIAN RIVER

The lovely Indian River is a short, three-mile-long stream flowing into Lake Muskoka from Lake Rosseau. Halfway up is a large pond known as Mirror Lake. Beyond that is Foreman's Narrows, named after a prominent family of settlers near Port Carling. The Foremans developed two resorts on the west side of the river: Endiang (later Arcadia Lodge) and Havington Inn. On the east side is a popular trailer park known as Glenwood.

The Nipissing II (Segwun) *docked at Port Carling, c. 1910.* NAC

The Sagamo *docked at Port Carling, c. 1900.* NAC

PORT CARLING

The charming village of Port Carling is appropriately known as the Hub of the Lakes. Originally called the Indian Village or Baisong (thunder-lightning) Rapids, it was named for Sir John Carling of London, Ontario, who as Ontario Minister of Public Works was largely responsible for having locks built here to bypass the rapids and allow steamers to navigate directly to Lake Rosseau.

The first European settlers arrived at Port Carling in 1865. Six years later the first locks were completed. Gradually a small village emerged, with stores and a few sawmills. As tourism began to replace lumbering on the local scene, the community flourished and developed five resort hotels plus several boatbuilding shops. Steamers called several times a day. In 1953 the locks were electrified, thus reducing the time required for locking through from half an hour to ten minutes. Today the village has a substantial business section, three churches, two marinas, and a museum. Population: c. 750.

Port Carling looking north, c. 1900. NAC

21. MINNEHAHA BAY

Minnehaha (laughing water) Bay is on the upper Indian River, directly above the Port Carling locks. About a mile upstream lies Lake Rosseau.

LAKE ROSSEAU

Lake Rosseau, the second of the three major Muskoka lakes, is 742 feet above sea level (three feet higher than Lake Muskoka). It stretches for a total length of about sixteen miles, terminating at Rosseau, and contains about seventy islands, of which one, Tobin Island, has a length of nearly three miles. The maximum depth is 295 feet. The lake takes its name from Jean-Baptiste Rousseau, a French-Canadian fur trader who frequented this area in the early nineteenth century.

22. FERNDALE HOUSE

On the south shore of Lake Rosseau stands the derelict hotel known as Ferndale House. First opened in 1880 by Richard Penson of Port Carling, Ferndale was sold to the Canadian Keswick Conference Society in 1926. In 1945 the main hotel was destroyed by fire, but it was rebuilt and enlarged and carried on until 1976, when the owners went bankrupt. Today the property remains vandalized and neglected. Close by are the old Port Carling fire tower (which offers a magnificent view of Lake Rosseau), the Muskoka Lakes Golf and Country Club (which has hosted many a boating regatta), and Shamrock Lodge.

View from Ferndale House, Lake Rosseau, c. 1906. NAC

Windermere House, Lake Rosseau, c. 1900. NAC

WINDERMERE

The small resort village of Windermere on eastern Lake Rosseau takes its name from Lake Windermere in northwestern England. It was first settled around 1868, and became a steamer stop the following year. The village really came to life around 1883, when Thomas Aitken, a Scottish settler, began enlarging his home to take summer guests. Within a few years his boarding house became Windermere House, which by 1887 was taking one hundred guests. Ten years later it was handling twice that number. Numerous other resorts soon followed, including the Fife House, the Maple Leaf House (now the Baldwins), King's Park, and Rostrevor Lodge, located on a lovely beach about two miles north.

In 1924 Windermere became an incorporated village. Of all its former resorts, only the Baldwins and Windermere House survive. Windermere House has just been meticulously rebuilt in the old style, following a tragic fire in February 1996. The village also has a store, post office, marina, golf and country club, and a garden centre, but no cemeteries. It is said to be such a healthy place that no one ever dies there! Population: c. 170.

23. WIGWASSAN POINT

Wigwassan Point, on eastern Tobin Island just north of Windermere, was once the lofty site of Wigwassan Lodge, one of the finest resorts on Lake Rosseau. Founded in 1905, the hotel was originally called Waskada Lodge, and later Epworth Inn, before becoming Wigwassan (silver birches) in 1932. It flourished until the 1950s, but finally deteriorated, and was closed and demolished after 1960. A gazebo and part of the old hotel wharf still survive.

Guests at Waskada Lodge, later renamed Wigwasson. NAC

Royal Muskoka Wharf, c. 1910. NAC

24. ROYAL MUSKOKA POINT

Royal Muskoka Point (sometimes called Royal Muskoka Island) was originally Wrenshall's Point, until the Muskoka Lakes Navigation Company bought it in 1901 and began erecting the Royal Muskoka Hotel, then the largest and grandest summer resort in all of Canada. Designed by expert architects, it had a giant, three-storey rotunda with spacious balconies flanked by two towers and two huge dormitory wings. Every possible

amenity was provided, including riding stables and a nine-hole, watered golf course. At its height the great hotel took 350 guests.

The Royal Muskoka began to decline during the Great Depression, but survived until the night of May 18, 1952, when fire destroyed it. The site has since been subdivided for cottages. The old hotel water tower still stands.

Royal Muskoka dining room. NAC

25. SKELETON BAY

Skeleton Bay, with Monyca Island at its mouth, is a lovely narrow arm of Lake Rosseau. It takes its name from the Skeleton River, which flows into the bay from Skeleton Lake, which now fills an ancient meteor crater. The name is said to have originated long ago when the skeletons of a native woman and her son who starved to death were found at a native campsite.

25. ROSSEAU FALLS

Rosseau Falls, where the Rosseau River spills down into the lake, was once a small lumber village. It was created around 1878 when Herman Muchenbaker built a sawmill there, along with shops, a store, docks, a school, and houses for his millhands. Like many another Muskoka lumber town, the village disappeared with the mill.

ROSSEAU

The village of Rosseau is an incorporated community at the head of Lake Rosseau. Originally called Helmsley, it emerged after the Parry Sound Road, running between Parry Sound and Falkenburg (north of Bracebridge), touched the tip of the lake in 1864. In 1870 William H. Pratt, a flamboyant Yankee, built the Rosseau House (commonly called "Pratt's Hotel"), the first wilderness resort in all of Canada, on a hilltop

The village of Rosseau, c. 1910.
Steamers Sagamo, Medora *and* Nipissing *at dock. The Monteith House stands at the left.* NAC

St. John the Baptist Church, Morinus. NAC

facing directly down the lake. Although it stood for only thirteen years before fire levelled it, Pratt's hotel became the forerunner of scores of other grand hotels in Muskoka. In the days before the railways Rosseau was also a major transshipping centre where people and goods were transferred from steamers to stages bound for Parry Sound and Lake Nipissing. In the 1890s it became a major resort centre, with over six hotels, including the Monteith House, Rossmoyne House, and the Maplehurst Hotel, none of which survive today. Today the village is a local service centre. Population: c. 200.

27. MORINUS

Morinus, on the northwest side of Lake Rosseau, was once the site of the Morinus House, a resort run by William D. McNaughton, starting around 1895. Today the site is occupied by Camp Nufrienda, which is owned by a group of Seventh Day Adventists. Close by is the old Roman Catholic church of St. John the Baptist, built by McNaughton in 1901 and still a major landmark on Lake Rosseau.

27. LAKE ROSSEAU BEACH RESORT

Lake Rosseau Beach Resort, formerly Paignton House, was founded by a settler named John Fredrick Pain and his family in 1895. They named it after their old home in England. It grew steadily, eventually taking one hundred guests, and remained a family enterprise until recent years. Unlike many other Muskoka resorts it is still in business today, and boasts its own golf course. It was renamed in 1996.

Clevelands House, Minett.
Steamer Medora *at the wharf.* NAC

29. CLEVELANDS HOUSE

Clevelands House, at Minett on western Lake Rosseau, is one of the loveliest resorts on the Muskoka lakes. Like most of the old hotels it began as a settler's farm, until the owner, C. J. Minett, saw the trends of the times and began taking guests at his home during the 1880s. From these beginnings Clevelands has blossomed into a grand hotel, noted especially for its tennis courts, golf course, and water-ski school. It can accommodate up to 350 guests. Immediately south of Clevelands House is Lakeside Lodge, a small, intimate family resort established in 1946.

Woodington House dock, Lake Rosseau, c. 1910. NAC

29. WOODINGTON HOUSE

The old Woodington House was located on a lofty hilltop about three miles south of Minett. It was founded in 1892 by an English settler named Michael Woods and once took 120 guests. Unlike Muskoka's other resorts, it was never seriously altered or modified in later years (except for the addition of electricity) and grew more and more dated; nonetheless, it continued to take guests until 1973. Subsequently it became a large summer cottage, though because of its size and the fact that it was often empty, the locals called it the "ghost hotel." In 1997 the historic structure was demolished by a wealthy Torontonian to make way for a new private retreat.

30. THE JOSEPH RIVER

The Joseph River forms the natural link between Lake Rosseau and its western twin, Lake Joseph. It once contained strong rapids, before the levels of the two lakes were equalized in 1871. Near the mouth of the river stood the former Nepahwin-Gregory Hotel, said to have been the first in Muskoka to feature electric lights. Nepahwin-Gregory closed around 1960 and no longer stands.

PORT SANDFIELD

The tiny village of Port Sandfield grew around a short canal cut in 1870–71 across a sandy isthmus separating Lakes Rosseau and Joseph. Premier John Sandfield Macdonald of Ontario visited the scene in 1870, and the site was named in his honour. As the new gateway to Lake Joseph, Port Sandfield saw a lot of boat traffic, but it really came to life in 1882 when Enoch Cox, a local settler, built the Prospect House hotel, directly facing the canal. It grew rapidly, soon taking two hundred guests, and was especially favoured as a sportsmen's haven. Four smaller hostelries also appeared nearby.

Although the Prospect House went up in flames in 1916, Port Sandfield is still noted for its church, four stores, and swing bridge (newly replaced in 1998). The tiny village boasts the largest marina on the Muskoka lakes. Population: c. 50.

Prospect House, Port Sandfield, c. 1900. Lake Joseph is on the left, Lake Rosseau is on the right. NAC

Elgin House in its heyday. The Lake Joseph Club now occupies this site. NAC

LAKE JOSEPH

Lake Joseph is the smallest (and perhaps the prettiest) of the major Muskoka lakes. It is about sixteen miles in length by four miles at its greatest width and contains about seventy islands. Named for the father of Jean-Baptiste Rousseau, who gave his name to Lake Rosseau, Lake Joseph has remarkably clear waters, being entirely spring fed. Its maximum depth is 305 feet.

32. THE LAKE JOSEPH CLUB

The new Lake Joseph Golf and Country Club lies adjacent to Port Sandfield across Cox Bay. For a century the site was occupied by the Elgin House, a splendid resort founded by Lambert Love in 1894. At its height the Elgin House almost eclipsed the Royal Muskoka. It was closed in 1993 and soon afterwards demolished, but the golf course has been rebuilt and was recently declared "the best new resort golf club in Canada."

33. PINELANDS RESORT

Pinelands, at the southern end of Lake Joseph, was originally two separate resorts: Pinelands Lodge, which was founded by J. H. Jones in 1906; and the Belmont House, established four years earlier by W. H. Fairhall. The two hotels were merged in 1942, under the name of Pinelands. (The existing hotel today is actually the former Belmont.) Rejuvenated during the 1980s, Pinelands is a delightful family resort and boasts the finest beach on Lake Joseph. In recent years it has again become a steamer calling place, with the *Segwun* stopping regularly on her 100 Mile Cruise.

34. MARYGROVE

The giant complex known as Marygrove, facing the former Elgin House, was originally the Glen Home Hotel, and was founded by the indefatigable Lambert Love around 1946, after his retirement from the Elgin House. Today Marygrove is a summer retreat, belonging to the Sisters of St. Joseph. Close by stood the Northernaire, a hotel that lasted only seven years before it went up in flames in 1960.

Belmont House, now Pinelands Resort. NAC

34. SHERWOOD INN

The Sherwood Inn is a beautiful year-round resort with a homey, English atmosphere. It was founded in 1939 and is noted as an ideal winter destination for cross-country skiiers. One of its outbuildings is called Edgewood and it occupies the site of a small housekeeping resort of that name, run by a Miss James at the turn of the century. Sherwood Inn still enjoys the occasional visit from the *Segwun*.

Foot's Bay. OA

35. REDWOOD

The former postal settlement of Redwood on southwestern Lake Joseph owes its name to the red maples that were once abundant in the area. During the 1890s it was also an important source of tanbark, which was cut by farmers from hemlock trees and scowed by tugs to the tanneries at Bracebridge for tannin. In later years a cabin resort was opened at Redwood; today the cabins are individually owned.

FOOT'S BAY

Foot's Bay, on western Lake Joseph, was named for an English gentleman named William Edward Foot, who arrived in 1869 hoping for a new life as a transplanted country squire. He quickly despaired of the rigours of pioneering in the Muskoka bush and moved to Bracebridge. One of his sons, Hamilton Foot, became a steamship captain, first on the Muskoka lakes and later on the Pacific. Foot's Bay is noted today mainly for its fine marina, recently renovated.

36. YOHO ISLAND

Yo-ho-cu-ca-ba Island is the most famous on Lake Joseph, in that it was selected as the headquarters of the Muskoka Club, a group of sportsmen from Toronto who were first attracted to Muskoka as early as 1860. The island took its name from the first syllables of the surnames of the founding members, one of whom was Professor John Campbell of McGill University, a once noted clergyman and classical scholar. A mysterious, ruined log house with trees growing through it was discovered on the island in the 1860s; it was said to have been built by a fur trader in the 1820s.

Professor Campbell's summer home, Yoho Island. NAC

37. THE CNIB CAMP, BARNESDALE

Lake Joseph Station

The Canadian National Institute for the Blind established its summer camp about a mile north of Foot's Bay around 1960. To the old-timers, however, the site is still Lake Joseph Station, a former railway depot opened by the Canadian Northern Railway in 1907 to allow passengers to connect with the local steamers. The Canadian Pacific Railway, whose tracks are adjacent, built its own station, called Barnesdale. Lake Joseph Station was demolished around 1957.

Canadian Northern Railway's Lake Joseph Station at Barnesdale, c. 1910. Steamers Sagamo *(behind the train) and* Ahmic *at the wharf, plus a yacht.* NAC

38. STANLEY BAY

Stanley Bay, in northeastern Lake Joseph, was named for the Stanley House, a resort hotel built in 1888. After the Summit House at Port Cockburn burned, Stanley House became the northern terminus for the steamers on Lake Joseph. The original hotel burned in 1920; the successor building still stands, and forms part of a Jesuit boys' camp known as Camp Ekon. The wreck of the steamer *Kenozha*, which burned one night in 1918, still lies in Stanley Bay.

39. ROCKY CREST

Hamer Bay, in northwestern Lake Joseph, is the home of the Rocky Crest Resort, which was founded in 1985. The *Segwun* has made the occasional visit to Rocky Crest.

Port Cockburn, c. 1910. Summit House stands to the left of the steamer wharf. Fraser Island is at the right. NAC

PORT COCKBURN

The former village of Port Cockburn stood at the northern tip of Lake Joseph. Named in 1872 for A. P. Cockburn, founder of the Muskoka Lakes Navigation Company and afterward Muskoka's first member of parliament, Port Cockburn, like Rosseau, became an unloading point for freight and passengers headed from the steamers to stages bound for Parry Sound. That year Hamilton Fraser began building the Summit House, the oldest resort on the Muskoka lakes, next to Pratt's

at Rosseau. Port Cockburn soon sprouted docks, a store, church, post office, telegraph office, and a boat livery, while the Summit House expanded to take two hundred guests.

In 1906 the railways bypassed Port Cockburn in favour of Barnesdale, or Lake Joseph Station. Then the Summit House burned in the fall of 1915, and the village became a ghost town. The historic site has occasionally been revisited by the RMS *Segwun* in recent times.

ABOUT THE RMS SEGWUN

Type:	Passenger twin-screw steamship (Daytime observation type)				

History:

1887	Built at the Clyde Shipyards, Scotland
1887	Assembled at Gravenhurst, Ontario
1887–1925	Original name: *Nipissing (II)*
1924–1925	Rebuilt at Gravenhurst
1887–1914 *and*	
1925–1958	In commission
1962	Converted into a museum
1969	Restoration commenced
1981	Restoration completed
1981	Returned to active service

Port of registry:	Toronto
Home port:	Gravenhurst
Length between perpendiculars:	121.0′
Length overall:	125.0′
Beam:	21.8′
Hold depth:	8.1′
Draft:	6.0′
Gross tonnage:	271.59
Register tonnage:	168.39
Hull construction:	Iron
Superstructure construction:	Wood

Hold bulkheads:
    1925, 1; c. 1947, 2; 1979, 4

Decks: Main deck, promenade deck (full length), and hurricane deck

Build:	Carvel

Stern:	Round fantail
Masts:	1
Lounges:	2
Dining Room:	1 (capacity c. 34)
Galley:	1

Staterooms: c. 1942, 2;   1946, 7;   1976, 0

Stairwells: 1925, 2;   1946, 1;   1979, 2

Engines: 2 fore-and-aft compound steam

High pressure cylinders:	10″ diameter
Low pressure cylinders:	20″ diameter
Length of stroke:	14″

Manufactured by Doty Engineering Works, Goderich, Ontario, 1907 and 1914 respectively

Boiler: 1 Scotch-Marine (fire-tube); 2 furnaces, hand stoked

Length:	10′
Diameter:	9.6′
Operating pressure:	160 lb./sq. in.

Manufactured by Engineering & Machine Works Ltd., St. Catharines, Ontario, 1925

Auxiliary Equipment:
    1 jet-condensing air pump,
    1 two-stage feedwater heater,
    1 independent duplex-boiler feed pump

Fuel:	Anthracite coal
Speed:	c. 12 knots
Crew:	Captain, mate, engineer, stoker-oiler, purser, deck hand, catering staff